LONG HAUL

Global Airlines
and their
Aircraft

LANCE COLE

Motorbooks International
Publishers & Wholesalers

DEDICATION

To the memory of Ernest K. Gann and his incredible words, without which I would not have flown this far.

Front Cover
KLM's mighty 747-400 *Melbourne* ready for ease back from her gate at Amsterdam Schiphol.

Rear Cover
BACKGROUND:
As dawn breaks over Siberia, this long haul jumbo is bathed in a curious pink light.

TOP:
Awaiting start-up, the big one, the 747-400 seethes with intent at the ramp.

BOTTOM:
American operate both DC-10 variants and also the MD-11. In the all-metal finish that these shots depict, the structural keys of the airframe are easy to spot.

Title Pages
One of Cathay's workhorse Tristars seen spooling up.

Air France Concorde captured on finals with the nose drooped and the sink rate arrested by thrust and the magic of the delta wing. This one is settling, swanlike, into Paris, Charles de Gaulle.

AUTHOR'S NOTE

Photographing aeroplanes is a passion enjoyed by many. I am lucky enough to have achieved publication of the airliner photographs that I have created whilst being part of worldwide airline operations. Airlife has previously published a series of top quality airliner books and it is, through *Long Haul*, my privilege to join their ranks.

Flying the great airlines on the great long haul routes has been the fulfilment of a childhood ambition. I grew up travelling on the dark blue-and-gold-liveried BOAC VC-10s with their supremely elegant design; I flew on the pristine, kingfisher-blue-hued KLM DC-8s with their professional, historical airs and graces allied to the best time-keeping. Trips on friendly Pan Am 707s, flights on Caravelles, Viscounts, and on Dakotas over Africa imbued in me a love of airliners that came to rule my life. I hope my enjoyment of great airliners has been captured in my photographs, and that you can share that as you journey through the book and its great long haul journeys around the airline world upon the wings of some great global airliners and their great airline moments.

All the photographs in *Long Haul* were taken by me en route around the world. With their rare access to flight decks and ramps, these photographs are the real thing, in-service, in-action and were taken with the help of many airline crews and airline people who are also captivated by flying.

With these photographs, I have tried to convey the magic of airline operations and the special flying feelings that they invoke. Whether it was standing under a 747 on the Hong Kong ramp as storm clouds cleared, accompanying a captain doing 'walk around' checks on the Amsterdam Schiphol apron amid the bright blue of KLM, or freezing on Chicago O'Hare's snow-lashed ramp as a DC-10 'heavy' thundered past, the moments have been wonderful memories. I have seen sunrise and sunset from behind the armour-plated wraparound windscreens of a 747 amid the cloudscapes of the globe, and never ceased to marvel at the moment. My cameras were always there and in *Long Haul*, the pick of these airline industry moments are presented in a manner not previously seen before. All the material was shot as it happened, nothing has been staged.

I hope this book will be enjoyed by everyone who is an airline enthusiast.

ACKNOWLEDGEMENTS

With thanks to all who have helped, notably:
Qantas — the crews, and the PR folk in London (Jane Ritchie), Sydney (David Rowley).
KLM Royal Dutch Airlines — all the crews I know, and the Schiphol head office PR team with Hans Leijte.
Cathay Pacific in Hong Kong (David Bell) and in the air.
American Airlines — on 'heavy' wings and at O'Hare field.
British Airways, Singapore Airlines, Garuda Indonesia, and Japan Airlines.
Canon Cameras Professional Services UK.
Fuji. Kodak.
Schiphol Airport Authority.
Boeing in London and Seattle.
Airlife for understanding airliners.

INTRODUCTION

This book takes you into the heart of today's airline operations the world over. The author's camera zooms in on classic, long haul jetliner moments with some of the leading airlines who gave the author unrivalled access to the flight decks, ramps, and runways of front-line airline life. The photo-story charts the great moments from some great airline journeys as seen from the flight deck and from the passengers' perspective. For airline enthusiasts, the 'live' action from the captain's seat is the real thing. The sheer breadth of the action covers Asia, Australia, Europe, Africa, and, of course, America. It includes airframe, engine and livery highlights as well as take-off and landing action captured from the flight decks of 747s worldwide.

Alongside the 747 family – the mainstay of airline life – there are sequences on the big twins and tri-jets that span the world's airways. The story takes you close up to in-service airliners and features rarely portrayed action the world over: pushback, start-up and slat selection, it's all there alongside shots of airline action at flight level three seven zero, cruising at Mach point eighty-five! Also depicted are worldwide airline moments as seen from the ramp at some of the world's great airports where, with privileged access, the camera has been able to capture the essential spirit of airline operations.

This book is not a reference work; instead, it is a combination of flying fact and flying feeling. It covers much airspace and takes the reader on a journey into the airline world; therein lies its appeal. For the author, the chance to photograph in-service operations with great airlines was a privilege extended to few; hundreds of hours on flight decks and dawn to dusk days out on the 'airside' tarmac of the world's airports were moments to be treasured.

Photographed using Canon cameras and a mix of Fuji and Kodak professional films, the book and the great airline moments it captures would not have been possible without the help and enthusiasm of airline and airport people all over the world; my thanks to them.

Long Haul is a colourful record of today's great airline routes and the machines that fly them. It is a unique journey on the wings of world airline operations.

Lance Cole

LEFT:
A magnificent Indian cloudscape rising to meet this 747-400 at flight level 350.

ABOVE:
A Cathay Tristar descends on its final approach into Hong Kong.

The fleeting shimmer of a red Qantas tail
as it flashes behind an Air Nauru 737
awaiting a night departure from Sydney.

South African Airways 747-300 *Cape Town* in pristine condition as she is towed to her gate for boarding.

OVERLEAF:
The business end of Boeing's biggest – the flight deck of a British Airways 747-400 en route LHR-HKG non-stop. The five CRT screens appear particularly clearly in this photograph taken as the Captain enters new data into his flight computer system.

QANTAS

One of the airline 'greats', Qantas was one of the first airlines in the world. After the Dutch carrier KLM, Qantas is the oldest airline in the world, having been founded in November 1920.

Under the guidance of early Australian aviation pioneers like Hudson Fysh, P.J. McGinnes, A. Baird and many other men with a belief in themselves and air travel in their emergent nation, Qantas has forged an enviable reputation. Originally founded as Queensland and Northern Territories Aerial Services (hence its acronym Qantas), the airline's first home base was at Longreach in northern Queensland. From there the early Qantas craft served the outback farming and mining settlements, expanding southwards to serve the nation's growing cities.

In the 1920s the early Qantas operations were based out of a wooden barn at Longreach where horses were tied up outside and de Havilland biplanes rested in the heat between outback sorties. The early Qantas days were of hand-pumped fuel, outdoor maintenance, and pioneering excavations in the bush to build runways and fuel stores. The airline's founders often went out into the back of beyond to survey and build their own facilities. Using the war surplus Avro 504, BE2, and de Havilland machines, the early Qantas days were of string, canvas, and wire-braced open cockpit aircraft and few navigational aids. Routes to towns and villages such as Toowoomba, Charleville, Blackall, Mount Isa and Darwin were the core of the 1920s Qantas development, yet as early as 1930 Qantas had set its sights on an international network – with visions of linking up with the Empire routes to England.

Thus, Qantas Empire Airways, driven by the Empire enthusiasm of its chairman Fergus McMaster, set about becoming part of Britain's Empire service by linking the Singapore end of the British Imperial Airways route in a partnership that flew initially to Brisbane and, later, onwards to Sydney. From 1934 to 1938, the QEA branch of the Qantas tree served this international route using the four-engined DH 86 biplane; then the elegant Shorts S. 23 flying boats arrived on the scene and began another chapter – which culminated in the famous Rose Bay flying boat base days, near Sydney. These machines, which cruised at 165 mph and carried fifteen passengers and a freight load, conveyed an incredible 5,000 passengers in their first nine months of operation.

The outbreak of the Second World War saw the cessation of the Empire connection via Singapore, but Qantas managed to run an Indian Ocean connecting service and began to look towards the Pacific whilst still maintaining its historic homeland operations; the mainstay of both these routes was the Consolidated PBY Catalina flying boat. The airline continued to use de Havilland, Handley Page and Armstrong Whitworth aircraft on its internal operations. However, the war created new perspectives for Australia and its airline. By the war's end, Qantas had access to Lockheed 10s, Douglas C-47s and a fleet of converted Liberator and Lancaster bombers with which it recommenced its long haul routes. Within five years of the war's end, Qantas had both established its American, pan-Pacific operations and re-established its old Empire networks, although on a far more independent basis.

Using the Lockheed Constellation, Qantas forged ahead on the so called 'Kangaroo' route to London. The journey was an advance on the old flying boat route, but it still took fifty-five hours to complete the 12,000 miles between Australia and England. Along the way the 'Qantas Connie', as it was known, stopped at Darwin, Tengah, Dum Dum, Karachi, Cairo, and then across Europe to London Heathrow.

The mainstays of the Qantas Pacific and Asian fleets were the Douglas DC-4, Lockheed Electra, and 0749 and 1049 Super Constellations. At the same time Qantas and its various arms were still using DH Beavers, Otters, Drovers and C-47/DC-3 marques to serve their diverse destinations, which included Java, Papua New Guinea, and, of course, the towns and strips of Australia's outback. This diversity of aircraft type requirement graphically illustrates the operating conditions of the varied Qantas routes. The creation of the DH Drover by adding a third, central engine to an existing airframe, increased the power and payload capacity in a way that enhanced the aircraft's 'outback' capabilities in a uniquely Australian way.

Having briefly flirted with a jointly titled BOAC/QANTAS Bristol Britannia and Comet service on the 'Kangaroo' route, Qantas entered the jet age for real in July 1959 when its first pure jet 707-138 entered service – at a time when the Electra and Constellation were the core of a propeller-powered fleet that finally signed off in 1964. By then Qantas had created a fleet of turbofanned, short-fuselaged 707s that flew higher and faster than their competitors. Named the 'V' jets, these machines powered Qantas ahead on the international scene until the arrival of the 747 Jumbo jet in 1971 – in 747B model guise. Apart from their first 747s, the entire Qantas 747 fleet, in all its variations, was by the 1980s entirely Rolls-Royce-powered. The fleet mix included the 747-238, the shorter bodied 747SP, the 747 extended upper deck -338 model, and more lately the mighty 747-400 series – named the 'Longreach' class after the Qantas home town of 1920. 1985 saw the delivery of the first of an order for ten of the big twin 767s which Qantas use both domestically and internationally, notably at their Singapore and Bangkok hubs.

Today, the Qantas network covers forty international cities; it puts South Africa one stop away, Tokyo and Hong Kong at close reach and America's west coast a non-stop fourteen-hour 747-400 flight away on a daily basis. With code sharing and domestic and international alliances undertaken, the Qantas of the 1990s is as diverse as it was in 1935.

Qantas has set high standards in the industry and is the world's leading safety rated airline. The fleet is maintained and crewed to the highest standards and has many achievements to its credit. Perhaps the most notable example of the Qantas way is the record-breaking delivery flight that the first Qantas 747-400 undertook. The aircraft was VH-OJA and it flew non-stop from London Heathrow to Sydney Kingsford Smith with a special fuel load, twenty non-revenue passengers and air traffic control co-operation in a record time of just twenty hours, five minutes and nine seconds. It was the first time that the famous 'Kangaroo' route between England and Australia had ever been flown non-stop, and there was a huge contrast between this feat and the old days of the Empire service.

Normal commercial operations still only stop once en route between the two nations – in either Singapore or Bangkok – and, as with the non-stop Pacific flights, the 747-400 operates at its incredible near maximum weight of 394.6 tonnes. Perhaps it is these flights, the ones that transport over 400 people half-way across the globe in safety and Australian style, that underline the history and commitment of Qantas and its past achievements on the international aviation scene.

The Qantas fleet in 1950 comprised four Constellation 0749s, thirteen DC-3s, five DC-4s, three Lancastrians, four Catalinas, eleven DH 84s, two Liberators, and one DH 83. The Qantas fleet in 1994 comprised twelve Boeing 747-438s, six 747-338s, eight 747-238s, seven 767-238s and twelve 767-300s, with further 747-400 and 767 options. The airline's base is at Sydney; its callsign is 'QF'.

BELOW:
The last delicate moments of controlling
almost 400 tonnes of aeroplane to a precise
halt at its Sydney landing gate.

RIGHT:
Two resting Longreach class 747s at
Sydney – keeping their Qantas tails in the
air.

The unmistakable double-decked nose
section of the B747 series.

ABOVE AND LEFT:
The winglets of the 747-400 are six feet high and are of composite fibre construction. They are incorporated into the wing design to reduce tip-end vortices which result in drag and also to reduce air turbulence behind the aircraft.

Flight deck sequence. With its "glass" cockpit, the 747-400 heralded the CRT displays and EICAS systems of computerised flight decks and management systems. These photographs were taken on board the QF001 and QF002.

In the picture above, First Officer Birdsall and Captain Hughes are guiding the Longreach into Bangkok; the runway is visible through the right-hand windscreen.

RIGHT:
Speed, height, flight director and other navigational instruments are here shown in rare photographic clarity.

LEFT TOP:
In the eerie light of sunrise, the Captain is captured in command perspective.

LEFT BOTTOM:
Look carefully at the instrument details and you will see "live" readouts for engine pressure ratios, target speeds and altitudes as well as other essential 747-400 pilot information – all caught live and in service.

Powerpoint. The intake of a Rolls Royce RB211/524, four of which power each of the Qantas Longreaches. Each engine produces 58,000lb of static thrust and drinks 764 litres of fuel per minute at take-off power.

KLM ROYAL DUTCH AIRLINES

Founded in 1919, KLM Royal Dutch Airlines was the dream of one man, Dr Albert Plesman, a Hollander who, after the Great War of 1914–18, realised the significance of the aeroplane and its new place in the world. During KLM's founding days, he set up a small air services company at Schiphol near Amsterdam and set about proving the worth of aerial transportation to Europe's new order. He cleverly gained a royal charter from the Dutch monarchy and his fledgling company became the Koninklijke Luchtvaart Maatschappij, or Royal Dutch Airlines. With contracts for transportation and charter within Holland, and soon between Amsterdam, Paris, London and Copenhagen, KLM rapidly became (and remains) a national symbol, held in affection.

Using Fokker aircraft produced by fellow Hollander Anthony G. Fokker, Plesman and his KLM company roamed far and wide. His early days also saw the operation of de Havilland machines and early Douglas craft. KLM has operated every model of Douglas machine including the obscure, high-winged DC-5 and the latest MD-11. Painted up in traditional KLM blue, Fokker's twins and tri-motors roamed the world in KLM colours under the command of famous KLM names such as Smirnoff, Parmentier, Geysendorffer, Uys, Soer, Van Beukering, Grosfeld, and many others. With the DC-2 and later the DC-3, KLM's East Indies route became established on the back of the Fokkers' pioneering trailblazing down through Asia. At that time, no other airline offered such a mastery of speed and safety on the run. Amsterdam to Batavia (now Jakarta) in four days was the proud boast. En route KLM ran its own accommodation and servicing for its planes and their passengers and created a legend separate from the Imperial Airways British Empire service.

A great fan of the American airline world, Plesman used his contacts in America to assure that KLM got the best, fastest, and newest types. After the war he used the surplus DC-3/C-47 marque to great effect on KLM's network of European cities – still served today by 737s and formerly by DC-9s and Viscounts, all bearing the 'Flying Dutchman' logo.

Perhaps KLM's most famous era was its operations with the Lockheed Constellation. Using these elegant machines, KLM took on the world. It replaced its DC-4s and conquered the north and south Atlantic, as well as the Polar, Asian, and African routes. A daily departure upon the wings of a Connie to many of the world's great capitals was KLM's proud boast.

Considering that KLM's home base had been obliterated in the Second World War, this revival was no mean achievement. Schiphol had formerly been an inland sea which had been drained. Now, where sailing vessels once tacked with the winds, giant airliners ride the winds and line up for take-off on one of the six runways. What was a tented city has become one of the world's most modern airports where KLM's renowned high standards are honed. Over seventy-five years on, KLM's uninterrupted record of service, starting from those early days in The Hague and then Schiphol, represents a great aviation legend. During the last war, KLM continued operations from neutral Portugal and in the Caribbean territories. As former Dutch colonies gained independence, KLM assisted in the setting up of airlines to operate in its place. Thus the KLM touch can be felt far and wide.

Reflecting Plesman's early work with cargo, freight, and post, KLM's current fleet includes cargo 'combi' variants of the 747-400 alongside standard versions. Today, the KLM blue adorns a mixed fleet of Boeing, Douglas, Saab, and Airbus machines. Dutch domestic services have been absorbed into a KLM Cityhopper division.

Like Qantas, and one or two other airline 'greats', KLM's early days meant real pioneering stuff such as making fuel dumps, spares, carving out runways and negotiating natural hazards. Profits and losses have come and gone, and like others, today's KLM has been forced to build global alliances – in KLM's case a tie-up with American Northwest Airlines has been made – giving it internal access to the US and in turn, access to the European hubs for Northwest.

KLM's history is littered with records and competition. When the DC-2 named *Uiver* raced from Holland to Australia and came second only to a racing craft, everyone knew KLM meant business. This professionalism was later exemplified by the graceful DC-8 years at KLM. From the early -30 model through to the stretched -60 series, KLM's elegant DC-8s took the Dutch name to over fifty international destinations. Trimmed in white and blue with Dutch scenes depicted in the interior, the KLM DC-8s with Pratt & Whitney fan power were a familiar sight on every continent with a reputation for fine timekeeping and reliable service.

KLM waited for the 747-200 – the 'SuperB' model – and their first was named *Mississippi*. Switching to a General Electric powerplant on later 747 orders, KLM created its rare extended upper deck 747-2/300 conversions from original -200 airframes –adding the advantage of the longer upper deck. Then came the 747-400. KLM's five DC-10-30s are being replaced with the updated MD-11 derivative whilst the Airbus A310s continue on many routes. KLM flies to over seventy destinations and all her craft carry the name of a city, a river, or a famous figure.

The KLM of today is both privately and publicly owned and, despite the small size of The Netherlands and their population, KLM is, and always has been, a big name in flying. The Dutch seafaring and exploring tradition is underlined by the sheer vastness of KLM's route network, which touches every major city and continent. With a superb reputation for safety and reliability, KLM can truly be said to be the grand old character of the airlines whilst still being at the forefront of technological developments and design. The fleet comprises eighteen 747-400s, thirteen 747-300s, ten MD-11s (ordered), five DC-10-30s, ten Airbus A310-200s, thirteen 737-300s, five 737-400s, ten F 50s, twelve S 340/Bs, four F 28s, and four F 27s. The airline's base is at Schiphol airport, Amsterdam, The Netherlands; its callsign is 'KL/KLM'.

LEFT:
The extended 211-feet, sixty-five-metre span of the 747-400, capable of arcing through six feet in the cruise, is best shown in this colourful winglet portrait.

ABOVE:
Photographed under the 747-400's nose, the engines frame a departing KLM A310 as it slips across the ramp, or 'platform' as the Dutch call it.

RIGHT AND OPPOSITE:
Nose to tail. These two shots make the most of the KLM blue.

BELOW AND OPPOSITE:
Take-off sequence. Seen from the runway's
edge, this KLM 747-400 is raging along
towards its V1 and Vrotate speeds. Seen
from the side and then nose-on, the flexing
-400 wings are shown taking the strain. At
160 knots and with the EPR on the mark,
this blue bird is off on a long haul.

An excellent view of the flap settings on
take-off as this 747-400 takes to the air.

Around Europe, KLM has replaced its DC-9 fleet with big-fan-engined baby Boeings – the 737-300 and -400. Here Captain Kroon is taking some last minute information before departing for Brussels.

BELOW:
Roaring along, this KL DC-10-30 is butting a crosswind on its take-off run. Used on African and American routes it will be replaced by the MD-11. One of five in the KL fleet, it is named after a great composer; as the accompanying KLM shots depict, KLM names all its craft after something or someone.

ABOVE:
Time is money – a fast turnaround is essential for long haul aircraft. Many sophisticated vehicles are used to replenish passenger requirements and flight essentials in the brief time available between flights. Here a 747-300 takes on stores before departing from Schiphol.

RIGHT:
The 737 *Jan H. Van Linschoten* is run back before the CFM fans spin up and the slats and flaps pop out to the take-off setting. Baby Boeings work hard, and this will be the first of several flights of the day.

ABOVE:
The Flying Dutchman levels out from the steep descending turn in the approach to Hong Kong airport. The rain cannot be helpful on this difficult landing.

LEFT:
One of KLM's 747-300 EUDs basks at the gate whilst being loaded. Note the classic shape of the General Electric engine pods. Not long after this moment was captured, the Boeing departed Schiphol for Jakarta.

OVERLEAF:
A hive of activity at Schiphol in Amsterdam. The two airbuses in the foreground are overshadowed by the sheer size of the 747-400 behind them.

The Flying Dutchman

A310

CATHAY PACIFIC

The Cathay Pacific story is a unique and classic tale. No other airline boasts a history so diverse or unusual.

Amid the mess that was Asia after the Second World War, opportunity abounded for those with drive and initiative; Cathay was founded by two men who were in the thick of it. Amongst the growing trade links, amid the cargo and materials that became the lifeblood of Asia, Texan Roy Farrell and Australian Sydney de Kantzow got together and created an airline. From early charter days traversing the famous 'Hump' with war surplus supplies in war surplus aircraft, Cathay has gone on to become a big player on the international airline scene.

Cathay Pacific Airways was born in 1946 on the wings of a single, battered DC-3 named *Betsy*. From their Hong Kong base, Cathay's operations flew cargo and people throughout Asia and Australasia, reaching Sydney, Singapore, Manila, Bangkok, and other points in between. After less than two years in operation, Cathay had seven DC-3s and two Catalinas in a fleet that never rested and made the most of every commercial opportunity that could be found. These were days of tough travelling, infamous passengers, even more infamous cargoes and a swashbuckling attitude that only Hong Kong could have created. Nicknamed 'Syd's Pirates' the airline nevertheless boasted high technical standards and crews who had learned their craft flying into China in the early *ad hoc* days when Farrell and de Kantzow used Shanghai as a temporary base.

Cathay, despite its unconventional characters and cargoes, soon became a high profile operation that was well known and a rich picking for the vested colonial politics that the opportunities of Asia's arena created. Thus, as early as 1948, Cathay's founding fathers had to find a more conservative base if they wished to continue riding Hong Kong's wave. By the end of 1948, Cathay had been absorbed by one of the established powerhouses of the Empire, where, under the control of John Swire, the airline carved a groove that has led to today's network.

Under Swire Cathay made slow but steady progress in the scheduled market and made the most of the post-war shift from sea transport to air connections. Within ten years, Cathay was carrying 50,000 passengers and 550,000 kg of cargo on its networks. The airline joined the jet age as early as 1962 with Convair 880s to replace its mainstay Lockheed Electras, DC-4s and DC-6s. Cathay graduated from the Convair to the 707, and then to the Tristar before acquiring 747s in 1979 when it was carrying the sort of loads that would have seemed amazing to its founders.

Two of Cathay's greatest feats have been on long haul routes. After years of trying, after years of fighting off London-based opinions on Hong Kong, Cathay finally got the rights to operate between its home base and London Gatwick (latterly Heathrow). A route of equal, if not perhaps greater, economic significance has been Cathay's defeat of distance across the Pacific to the lucrative west coast of America.

Cathay's Rolls-Royce-powered fleet is perhaps best epitomised by the 747-400, although Cathay's ultra-long haul routes were pioneered by the 747-200B model. Both of these models of the mighty 747 are heroes on Cathay's CX800 flights that reach non-stop over the Pacific Ocean between Hong Kong, Vancouver, San Francisco, and, now, Los Angeles. The transpacific route is Cathay's blue riband operation that spans a fourteen-hour flight time through the night and over the dateline. The 747-400 takes a 'great circle' route up over the ocean, skims Japan's eastern shores and then turns right up toward the Aleutian Islands before passing its point of no return. Then the fuel-laden, near 400 tonne giant scythes through the Pacific night and carves into California. In the Boeing's belly, over 400 passengers feed and sleep, all of which is a long way from the days when a stained DC-3 with bench seats and boxes of cargo strapped to the floor chugged across Asia on Cathay's early services.

The Cathay of today is that of a respected international carrier that reflects its Asiatic roots but which looks both east and west from its Kai Tak base. The fleet includes thirteen 747-400s, six 747-300s, six 747-200s, three 747-200Fs, two 747-400Fs, eight Tristars, to be replaced by ten Airbus A330s. The airline's base is at Kai Tak, Hong Kong; its callsign is 'CX'.

A 747-300 captured against the mountainous background of the approach to Hong Kong airport.

From the captain's seat. This is the real thing. The analogue instruments of a 747-200 on the CX800 fourteen-hour ultra-long haul run from Hong Kong to San Francisco captured from the left-hand commander's seat; the jumbo was mid-Pacific at the time.

The ever-busy flight engineer and his panel is seen accompanying the moment.

RIGHT TOP:
Rather like long-range homing pigeons –
our recently arrived 747 nestles into line
with other members of the Cathay flock.

RIGHT BOTTOM:
Passengers disembarking into waiting
coaches in Hong Kong's Kai-Tak airport.

BELOW:
Cathay Pacific 747-300 with all her
landing flaps extended, roars overs the
threshold seconds before touchdown at
Kai-Tak.

Cargo containers being put aboard this 747-400 on the ramp at Kai-Tak.

BELOW:
Spotters' delight! This 747-400 was on lease from Air New Zealand – hence the hybrid livery captured on the Kai Tak ramp. An impressive airline moment.

Another Cathay workhorse – a Tri-Star, here seen spooling down.

Cathay's Rolls-Royce-powered fleet are kept very clean. Here the 'RR' legend is framed by the author's intimate proximity to the business end of an RB211-524 engine!

Ground staff tend a China Airlines 747-400 while it embarks passengers at its gate in Hong Kong.

Wearing the old Malaysian livery, this 737 has just packed away her reverse-thrust buckets and is braking through 50 knots on the slow down at Singapore Changi airport.

ABOVE:
Bali High. A new Garuda MD-11 skims onto the runway at Bali's beautiful Denpasar airport. 'Thrust Reverse' is about to be called.

LEFT:
Mandarin Airlines 747SP rolls in to Sydney in the early morning light on arrival from Taipei.

Philippine Airlines moment. An early
A300 takes on passengers at Tokyo Narita
prior to a full load, late night departure to
Manila.

Thai tailpiece. Thai's Airbus in purple and gold departs left to right at Kai Tak whilst the polka-dotted liveries of the ramp watch. Behind the JAL 'Ten' are some pretty spectacular cargo paint schemes.

BRITISH AIRWAYS

The name British Airways first took to the air as long ago as the 1930s. In between then and now, the title remained buried amid the shifting themes of British air transport history and its various incarnations.

Today's British Airways came into being in 1972 when, under Government decree, Britain's international flag carrier, BOAC, merged with the nation's domestic and European airline known as BEA. Thus, the British Overseas Airways Corporation (BOAC) and the British European Airways (BEA) became British Airways — and an amalgam of all that had gone before. Therein lay some of the problems that beset the carrier before it grew into today's front-line, world famous carrier.

In the heady days of pre-war Britain when the nation and its far-flung empire prospered, the economy supported dozens of small airlines that had ambitious dreams. Whilst some of those dreams became commercial nightmares, most of the airlines survived. Healthy competition and excellent aircraft ensured that places like Croydon aerodrome were the hub of a busy industry. From the one-man outfits, through the smaller airlines came the mergers that created the core of Britain's civil aviation heritage.

British Airways today stems from the founding of Imperial Airways back in 1924. Imperial, like KLM and Lufthansa, built upon the advances in aviation as a result of the First World War. Through the merging of Aircraft Transport and Travel, Handley Page Transport, Instone Airlines and Daimler Airways — all pioneers of early airline history — Imperial took to the air. It became famous first for its long haul Empire routes, and luxurious standards on board its Heracles and Hannibal class flagships. With de Havilland, Armstrong Whitworth and Handley Page machines in its fleet, Imperial spread its wings throughout the 1920s and the 1930s. During this period Imperial reached its technological peak with the introduction of Empire class S 23 flying boats on transatlantic, African, and Asian routes.

Imperial's excellent safety record started with the giant HP 42 class: with four engines and carrying thirty-eight passengers at a sedate 100 mph they flew over ten million incident-free miles on European, African, and Indian routes. These routes were carved out of difficult and often unexplored topography. Imperial's Shorts Calcuttas, Atlanta and Scipio classes became the mainstays of a fleet that operated in a unique manner. The airline built fuel dumps, aerodromes, navigation beacons and its own hotels along Empire routes that became the backbone of British influence abroad — the name 'Imperial' aptly fitted the age.

After the Second World War, circumstances changed and Imperial died at the hands of a British government intent on creating a nationalised airline structure. In its place came BOAC operating only on international routes, whereas the newly created BEA formed in 1946, served the nation's domestic and European airline needs.

Post-war, history repeated itself with British airlines using converted bombers as passenger-carrying craft. The Lancastrians and Yorks of BOAC kept the Empire routes alive before the DC-6, Hermes, Argonaut and Constellations arrived. The 'Kangaroo' Route to Australia developed apace, as did the Atlantic services.

1952 saw the first pure jet service in the airline world with the ill-fated DH Comet. The Stratocruisers of BOAC still traversed the Atlantic in style and became famous for their double-decked cabins. They were replaced by Super Constellations and the much delayed Bristol Britannia at a time when BOAC was suffering aircraft shortages as a result of the Comet's grounding. By the time the revised Comet appeared, the 707 had stolen the market and changed everything.

BOAC made a success of the Comet — it had to. That did not stop it buying 707s with which it competed against the Pan Am, TWA, Lufthansa, and Qantas machines on key routes. At the same time, and affected by politics, the Vickers VC 10 appeared upon the confused scene. It was designed to operate on 'hot and high' Empire routes and was thus equipped with clean, high-lift wings, four rear-mounted engines and a very strong structure. By the time it arrived, the Empire route runways had been lengthened in order to accommodate the 707 and DC-8. Thus the VC 10 had been handicapped; it was stretched into the more viable 'Super' version, but never achieved great sales. However, in BOAC hands it was successfully used on all the airline's worldwide routes where it became very popular with passengers, not least because of its smooth handling characteristics and supremely elegant swept-finned appearance. The VC 10 probably epitomised BOAC at its best and political worst, and it stayed in service until BOAC had become British Airways. By then, the corporation had become, by common consent, a sad reflection of a once glorious institution. It would not be until the airline was privatised that its standards of service returned to those of the highest.

All this took place against the backdrop of a merger between BOAC and BEA. BEA had come into being to service the growth of peacetime Europe. Drawing its routes from a cast of independent British airlines, BEA operated DC-3s in its early days. It went on to pioneer the famous Vickers Viscount and the Airspeed Ambassador. It even used the revised Comet 4 alongside Tridents and BAC 1-11s, aircraft that were conceived around BEA's needs. Throughout the 1950s and the 1960s, BEA held court over domestic and European routes alongside a number of growing independent airlines which even used ex-BEA Vickers Vikings to great competitive effect. BEA had begun its days as the nationalised face of British short haul operations, and ended them under similar Government orders in a merger with BOAC.

From 1976, the newly created British Airways went on to pioneer Concorde, the world's only scheduled supersonic airliner. It built up a fleet of Boeing 747s and absorbed British Caledonian and others. Revitalised in the 1980s, the privatised BA has gone on to build a huge fleet that now serves 150 cities on every continent. The fleet comprises seven Concordes, twelve 747-100s, twenty 747-200s, thirty 747-400s, twenty-seven 737-300-400s, fourteen 767-300ERs, thirty-six 757-200s, ten BAe ATPs, and ten Airbus A320s. They have orders for 767 and 777s. The airline's premier routes reflect its history: from Heathrow, its routes to New York, Tokyo, Singapore, Sydney and Johannesburg represent core, blue riband services, all of which connect with an extensive European network based upon BEA history. The airline's base is at London Heathrow; its callsign is 'BA/Speedbird'.

LEFT:
Cargo, Asia's lifeblood. Nippon Cargo Airlines 747 freighter steadies over the Kai Tak fence. The road signs mean this is Hong Kong!

PREVIOUS PAGES:
Over Kowloon, the BA 747-400 arrives non-stop from London. Note the flexing wings and sparkling paint job!

Clearly showing the extended upper deck design and winglet addition, this 747-400 is getting a push prior to start-up. Note the aerodynamically superior long engine cowling and pylon combination of the shorter-cored Rolls-Royce engine option.

Thunderbirds are go! Concorde leaps off 27 right as the re-heat echoes around Heathrow.

Caught on finals for a homecoming, the
setting sun greets BA's six pm arrival from
JFK. Note the engine intakes – beyond the
sound barrier their airflow is controlled by
ramp intake doors.

LEFT:
Classic detail. British Airways call their early generation 747s 'classic' – and rightly so. Here a Pratt & Whitney-powered 747-100 'classic' takes a rest.

BELOW:
Classic climb out. A British Airways 747 roars up from Heathrow's 27 right as the gear comes up.

51

Classic arrival. Flaps 25, 150 knots, spoilers armed: this 747 is twenty seconds from touchdown.

Some of the early BA fleet have been re-engined from Pratt & Whitney to Rolls-Royce RB/D4 powerplants. Here another BA 'classic' steadies on finals for 27 right.

OVERLEAF:
One of BA's 757 fleet sinks in on a winter's evening. It looks serene, but in fact the wake turbulence from this machine caused strong gusts around the cameraman!

GREAT AIRLINE MOMENTS 1

Air Zimbabwe's highly regarded operations feature 737, 767-200ER. BAe 146 and a couple of classic 707-300s. This is their Harare ramp scenery.

ABOVE:
An interesting line-up of VIP Flight machines frame this South African Airways 747 and her Pratt & Whitneys.

RIGHT:
A Saudia 747SP shows off her simplified flap system. Forty-three of these shorter, lighter 747 variants were built. The taller tail enhances the shorter fuselage's directional stability characteristics. If Boeing had added the extended upper deck, this might have been the world's first full-length double decker – as a 747SP EUD!

LEFT:
Spectacularly spotlighted by the setting sun, this Pakistan International 747-200 is awaiting line-up for take-off from London whilst the usual rush hour queue builds up.

BELOW:
Against a fiery sky, Kuwait Airways 747-200 steals up to hold, ready for take-off from Heathrow's 27 right en route to New York as smoke drifts on the horizon.

NorthWest's latest red seen as their code-shared, joint KLM service awaits departure to Minneapolis/St Paul from Schiphol Amsterdam.

AMERICAN WINGS

Whilst Europe in the early 1920s was expanding its airline networks, the American air transport scene remained in a state of *ad hoc*, haphazard development. Even in 1923, rail and road was the preferred U.S. transport option, yet, within a decade, the American airline network would race ahead and eclipse its worldwide competitors.

War surplus de Havilland D.H.4. biplanes were the mainstay of barnstorming maverick pioneers who traversed the United States attempting to persuade the public to take to the skies. However, the springboard of technical and commercial development offered by the indirect subsidy from the new U.S. Mail air service was the key to bringing America's aviation loose ends together in 1920. In the period 1920 to 1924, the air mail service grew from a daylight network, into a scheduled, reliable day and night express system that linked New York to San Francisco. The mainstay of this route was a beacon light airway across the country that was unique in the world and which gave birth to the great airline companies of today.

Small airlines bid for sectors on the government-run mail network and many fed upon each other. At their height, there were 420 separate airlines on the U.S. scene. Their downfall lay in a lack of integration and high overheads.

Major players included the Ford company who took on board William Stout's ideas for an all-metal airliner – which became the ubiquitous Tri-Motor – mainstay of the early networks alongside the Fokkers and Curtis machines. Even Boeing, the mighty plane maker has its roots in mail and passenger services using its own airliners such as the model -40 and later on the advanced -247.

The West coast saw the fastest development of aerial services. Western Air Express under Harris Hanshue put the Los Angeles route on the connecting map using Douglas M-2 biplanes. In similar vein, Varney Air Lines and Pacific Air Transport served the connecting networks of the expanding mail and passenger services.

In the Eastern U.S. airline development had been slower but caught up through the work of outfits such as National Air Transport and its founder Clement Keys. Others were Transcontinental, Eastern Air Transport, Maddux, Southern, Luddington, Boston-Maine and Pitcairn Airways.

Thus, through such mergers, the great American carriers were created. Today, just as it was over fifty years ago, American Airlines is arguably the typical example of an American airline 'great'. Having started out as American Airways, from the basis of a merger of twelve small regional airlines, which became the Aviation Corporation, and then the American Airways company, the airline has become America's biggest. Its success stems from a regional hub and spoke system that now extends to Europe as

No review would be complete without Pan Am. Here, one of their early 747-100s in the original livery, seen on finals towards the end of the Pan Am era. Whilst it might have lost the grace with which it started, it is still hard to believe that Pan American has gone.

well. American today has a fleet of approximately 630 aircraft, 95,000 employees serving 200 world cities and 2,480 daily departures. This massive undertaking best exemplifies the sheer scale and history of the American airline scene. Just as with Transcontinental and Western Airways (now TWA) and both United and the once great Eastern, American has its roots in the late 1920s emerging scene of the U.S. Mail service contracts, government regulations, the birth of the true airliner, and the vision and drive of a single personality at its helm.

It was these diverse corporate and political strings which having come together, meant that in one year – 1929, – 160,000 citizens travelled by air. Yet, the companies still existed on the back of U.S. Mail business. Matters came to a head when Walter Brown, U.S. Postmaster General re-shaped the entire industry. Brown decreed that new routes were to be served by single airlines not an *ad hoc* amalgam. This effectively killed off the myriad network of small airlines and saw the forming of the big four – the main players – Patterson's United, Rickenbacker's Eastern, Smith's American, and Frye's TWA. They, under the strong characters of their respective Presidents swallowed the entire system and carved it up between them, which resulted in a government enquiry. The fact remained however, that competition had bred competitive scheduled passenger services and given birth to Braniff and Delta.

As the 'thirties dawned, the days of Stearmans and D.H.4s, of forced landings and of parachute-clad passengers sitting upon mail sacks, were truly over. Tri-Motors, Curtis Condors, Boeings and Fokkers provided safe and comfortable scheduled services throughout America. Alongside the big four, there was also Pan American. Under the control of one man – Juan Trippe – Pan American Grace Airways, and New York, Rio and Buenos Aires Line became Pan American and reflected Trippe's international aspirations.

Trippe was born into the upper echelons of American society and he used his contacts to create an airline and gain U.S. government support. He also flew his own Fokker and Sikorsky aircraft on pioneering flights. Pan Am's early days used the international U.S. Mail subsidy to start up international routes – notably in the Caribbean and Latin America.

Trippe started with one route and within three years he had services to twenty countries and had, through his absorption of the NYBRA flying boat line, and his joining with the Grace company, a diverse network supported by mail contracts. In 1935, Trippe achieved his greatest feat with the starting of Pan American's Clipper flying boat service across the vast Pacific Ocean to Manila and beyond.

After the war, the airline world changed, and Pan Am's character had to change too. It went on to become a global great of the jet age. Few could have predicted the sad end that awaited Pan American when economic pressures bankrupted the great airline institution.

Despite their differing characters, all the American carriers shared an involvement in the design of their airliners. From the DC-1, DC-2, and DC-3, through to the jet age and the 707, DC-8 and 747, the airlines' requirements of range, payload and performance dictated the design direction of many models of American airliners. None exemplified this more than the involvement of the big four in the DC-1, DC-2 and the later DC-3 sleeper and mainliner models that totally eclipsed the competition and set a new world standard.

Today, the turbulent commercial realities of the airline world have seen the death of both Pan Am and Eastern, with others of

BELOW:
Guess where United have landed!

RIGHT:
United's new colours captured as an early 747 climbs out from Heathrow's runway 27 right. Those Pratt powerplants are really pumping!

the once great 'big four' also suffering economic difficulties. From the heady days of 1925 when 130 new airlines sprang up (rising to a short high of 420), there remains a core of U.S. airlines, most of whom can trace a lineage back to the early days. The sheer scale of American aviation is demonstrated by the huge fleets that the big carriers own, with a fleet mix of several hundred aircraft being common to each of the main carriers. This demonstrates the scale of distances inherrent in U.S. travel – where a domestic sector can, by European terms, be classed as a 1,000 mile long haul flight. Within the U.S. system there are routes that encounter high altitude runways, tropical and Arctic temperatures, and ocean crossings. This has resulted in long and short haul aircraft with two, three, and four engines and varying configurations. The 707, DC-8, 747, DC-10, MD-11, 727, 737 and DC-9/MD-80 are all American aircraft which reflect their domestic route needs as well as those of foreign markets.

The rise of the 'big twin' airliner such as the 767, 757 and latterly the giant 777 can also be linked to the operational needs of U.S. domestic and over ocean routes that cover long and mid range sectors where once the four-engined and tri-motor configuration ruled – as it had since the 1920s.

These routes are today operated by America's major airlines and reflect tradition in being fed at their major hubs by smaller 'feeder' carriers – encouraged by airline deregulation. The airline industry has changed, but the names have not. American, Continental, Delta, Northwest, TWA and United still represent the main players at domestic and international level. Within the U.S. an array of mid-sized and smaller carriers complete the scene, with the likes of Western, SouthWest, Alaskan, and U.S. Air being typical of the type.

The diversity of American operations was once best exemplified by Pan Am's round-the-world service, today, that scale of operation has gone, but the European hubs of American and United are testament to the operational strength of the U.S. airline industry's global scale and huge market. Whatever the changes, history remains a great influence. Whilst the days of the Lockheed Constellation, Boeing Stratocruiser and Douglas DC-6 and DC-7, may be over, many of the legendary liveries that adorned them, are still flying as American wings.

Today's American air includes the bold
livery of NorthWest. This new 747-400 was
shot on the ramp at Sydney.

ABOVE:
DC-10 study. NorthWest's glossy red looks pretty good on the angular lines of the Ten.

LEFT:
The Delta livery seen far from Delta's home. This is Bangkok at seven am, and the author snapped the impressive Delta MD-11 from the flight deck of another airline's 747-400 as it jogged up to the gate!

LEFT TOP:
Commuter America. This American Eagle-operated Shorts craft is moving out of O'Hare under the T tails of real Americana.

LEFT, BOTTOM AND BELOW:
American operate both DC-10 variants and also the MD-11. In the all-metal finish that these shots depict, the structural keys of the airframe are easy to spot.

Delta's 767 and crew at Frankfurt in this elongated shot that makes it hard to tell the 757 from the fatter 767.

BELOW:
Tow it away! The Frankfurt tow crew pull the Delta 767 up to the start point.

ABOVE:
The sagging fuel-laden wings of Air Canada's 747-400 hold alongside a United 747SP on a hot, thunderstormy day. A real moment of 747 anticipation and a super sensation for the photographer at the runway holding point.

LEFT:
United's 727 ramp at San Francisco. Here the 727s are edged by an elderly, long-body DC-8, and that's a 767 sneaking away in the mid-ground.

NorthWest rolls out. Seen in the interim livery of the post Northwest Orient days, this 757 is captured at Toronto as she takes off.

LUFTHANSA

Like British Imperial Airways, Deutsche Lufthansa came into being through the merger of early pioneering airlines set up after the First World War. 1919 saw the Deutsche Luft Reederei make early scheduled flights within Germany; at the same time, Rumpler Luftverkehr was also active as an early German airline. By 1926, these two and several smaller outfits had joined forces to become Deutsche Lufthansa – known today as Lufthansa.

Lufthansa's early routes were short haul within Germany; by 1930 it had an extensive intra-European network carrying passengers, freight and mail, much as KLM and Air France were doing. Just as Imperial was tied to the British aircraft industry and KLM was tied to Fokker, Lufthansa was from its inception tied to Junkers and Dornier. From early operations, the Junkers F 13 was a Lufthansa mainstay, its novel, all-metal cantilevered construction, corrugated skin, and four seats made it a safe, strong, 'high-cycle' performer.

Lufthansa expanded its wings and, using Dornier flying boats, made explorative journeys to South America in order to serve Germany's Latin American sphere of influence. This early experience was of great help when Lufthansa crossed the North Atlantic in 1936 with Dornier Do 18 flying boats. These giant machines took off from a lake near Berlin, set down near a refuelling ship in mid-ocean and then continued to New York. By this time the airline was serving much of Europe with Heinkel 111s and heading further afield with the elegant and advanced long range FW Condors.

Lufthansa's trans-ocean flights in the thirties with the giant Do X and the Junkers G 38 took design and capacity into a new age, but the advance in pure airline terms was curtailed by the advent of the Second World War. However, despite the constraints of post-war politics, Lufthansa took to the air again and did not forget its early history. Thus it is today possible to fly from the carrier's Frankfurt home base to South America and on over the Andes to Chile, as it was in the past.

Some of Lufthansa's greatest moments came from its exploits with the Junkers 52 tri-motor. The famous Junkers corrugated skin construction, full span flaps, wide undercarriage and reliable engines came together in the Ju 52 to create a workhorse machine that Lufthansa used not only in Europe but also further afield, notably in the tough South American conditions. In Europe, the Ju 52s carried the legend 'Lufthansa Berlin Tempelhof'; however, after the Second World War, it would be many years before Lufthansa made a return to its famous hub.

Today's Airbus A340s and Boeing 747-400s fly non-stop on these routes and others that were carved out by Lufthansa's Lockheed Constellations in the 1950s. The airline's routes to America, Africa, and the Far East are still its core themes. Thirty years ago they were served by the carrier's Boeing 707 aircraft; today both Boeing 747s and the twin-engined Airbus can be seen on these routes, including extended range trans-ocean routeings.

In Europe, Lufthansa is a premier business market carrier. The intra-European network was carved out with Boeing 737 and 727 aircraft in the 1960s, Lufthansa being the European launch airline for these aircraft. Today, Boeing 737-300, -400 and -500 series craft complement Airbus A320 machines on European sectors using Hamburg, Frankfurt and Munich as main hubs. Despite being an established 'great' in the airline world, Lufthansa has always been of an independent mind. In the past it soldiered on with Junkers 52s when all the world had access to the DC-3; today it designs its fleet and services to its own standards and ideas. The airline has a fine reputation for timekeeping, maintenance and safety. Lufthansa serves over one hundred and twenty destinations worldwide as well as having an extensive European network that incorporates regional and commuter carriers.

The famous flying 'crane' first appeared as Lufthansa's logo and remains so to this day, the company's trademark recognised the world over as the symbol of an historic airline institution. The fleet comprises eighteen 747-400s, ten 747-200s, four 747Fs, seventeen A340s, eleven A300-600s, fifteen A310-200/300s, thirty 737-300s, thirty-two 737-500s, thirteen 737-200s, forty-five A320s, and twenty A321s. The airline's base is at Flughafen, Frankfurt; its callsign is 'LH'.

The latest livery. Lufthansa's A320 curves into the stand under the command of the man in the left-hand seat.

OPPOSITE:
DC-10 moments. The famous 'crane' logo, has adorned every machine since the 1930s and the Junkers 52. These two were captured at the carrier's Flughafen Frankfurt base.

After the American operators, Lufthansa were the main 727 enthusiasts outside America. Operating early -100s and then the -200 series, their blue-tailed seven twos always looked smart and climbed steeply. This one is at Frankfurt by night.

ABOVE:
A340 arrival. Here, fresh in from South America, one of Lufthansa's latest long range wingletted wonders noses in to the stand. Note the high aspect ratio span and DC-8 style nose-down stance; max. all-up weight is 558,900 lb or 253,500 kg.

RIGHT:
A340 composite fibre tail frames the Frankfurt legend.

Lufthansa operates the whole 737 big fan family as well as the competing Airbus A320/21 to service the same routes. Here the -300 variant blasts up into European skies.

Sydney arrival. A big 747-400 moment this one. With a rainswept Sydney skyline, the Frankfurt–Sydney flight punts in with some style. A few more feet, ease back on the column and the big Boeing will settle down nicely.

JAPAN AIRLINES

Japan Airlines was born amid the rebuilding of Japan and its society under American administration after the Second World War. Thus it had access to the remarkable DC-3, with which JAL made its first tentative steps in early 1951. JAL was founded with private funding and began scheduled services linking Tokyo, Sapporo, Osaka and Fukuoka with leased aircraft and crew. By 1954, JAL's first international route to San Francisco via Wake and Honolulu using DC-6Bs was established. There had been airline operations within Japan prior to the war, but it took the single entity of JAL to build upon the need for air links that a fast growing Japan needed. JAL's progress was fast: by 1954 it had become a national institution under Japanese law as the Japan Airline Co. Ltd.

JAL's early fleet consisted of a mix of Douglas and Convair craft, some of which were built under licence in Japan at the factories of the former Japanese aircraft manufacturers. By 1960, JAL had entered the jet age with the arrival of its DC-8, which went into service on the Tokyo– San Francisco route. In 1962, JAL employed the Convair 880 to cross Asia on its 'Silk Road' service to Europe. At the same time, JAL inaugurated the Polar route with which it was to become well known.

There were many airlines who came to use the Polar shortcut via Anchorage in order to reach Europe, but it was the JAL DC-8s that really made it their own. From late 1961, JAL's spotless DC-8s jetted over the Pole to London and Paris. The elegant white-painted DC-8s became a JAL icon and culminated in the DC-8-63 series which was a favourite with passengers and crew alike. Alongside other Polar route pioneers like SAS and KLM,

JAL's Polar DC-8s became one of the airline world's great experiences of its time. Despite being supplanted in 1972 by the 747, the DC-8 days are still revered at JAL; such was the affection for the type that it remained on the fleet up until 1989. By then the JAL fleet included the DC-10, the 747 and the 767, and had the 777 on order. At that time JAL was the world's largest 747 operator with over fifty in the fleet; this included the domestic route optimised 747-SR with 550 seats! JAL's routes cover Asia, Europe, and America, and even reach down from Tokyo to Rio de Janeiro.

JAL's domestic routes have seen competition from other Japanese carriers, as, to a lesser extent, has its international operations. However, JAL's widely diversified corporate interests have underlined its strength. Perhaps its best known non-passenger activity is the JAL/JUST cargo system using a scheduled network of 747 freighters, covering sixty-four cities in twenty-nine countries. Other JAL offshoots include Japan Asia Airlines and the JAL Charter company.

Today, JAL serves over fifty international destinations and fifteen domestic cities. Tokyo Narita and Tokyo Haneda are the two main JAL home base hubs. The JAL fleet all carry the flying oriental crane, or 'Tsuru', upon their tails in the traditional JAL red and white colours, and the fleet, including options, is huge: it comprises seventeen 747-400s, thirty-four optional, nine 747-300s, twenty-five 747-100/200s, ten 747 SRs, ten 747Fs, seventeen DC-10-40s, sixteen 767-200/300s, ten MD-11s, ten optional and ten 777s on order. The airline's base is at Narita, Tokyo; its callsign is 'JAL'.

LEFT:
With Concorde passing by, an LH shuttle Airbus awaits taxi clearance from Heathrow ground control before departing for Munich.

ABOVE:
JAL's latest, the 747-400 at Hong Kong.

OPPOSITE AND ABOVE:
Tokyo by night as the big JAL 747 awaits
the author. Then it's a six-hour haul up to
Anchorage where, after an hour's rest, the
big Boeing hauls out over the frozen sea
and on over the scenic polar regions en
route to landfall in Paris after nine hours
on the wing.

OVERLEAF:
Tokyo Narita is JAL to the core. Here the
snow and the sun frame the flying stork
logo.

SINGAPORE AIRLINES

Officially, Singapore Airlines, or SIA as it is known, is only twenty-three years old, however, whilst the name Singapore Airlines was launched in 1972, the airline has roots in the Asian airline world that go back a lot further.

As part of the confederation of Malayan states, the first air services from Singapore were launched in 1947 under the Malayan Airways banner – an Airspeed Consul being used to connect Singapore with Kuala Lumpur, Ipoh, and Penang. From those early days and aircraft – that included the ubiquitous DC-3, a network of inter-state and inter-island services was built up. In 1963, the airline changed its name to Malaysian Airways. Then, in 1967, as the region's political map changed, it became Malaysia-Singapore Airlines. This company ceased operations in late 1972 and the independent Singapore Airlines was born.

Having entered the jet age in the late 1960s with leased Comets, SIA immediately embarked on the fleet renewal cycle for which it has become famous – consistently operating the world's youngest airline fleet. At its launch, the airline's ten aircraft linked twenty-two cities in eighteen countries. Today, SIA and its subsidiary, Silk Air, operate to eighty-seven cities in forty-two countries using a variety of airliners, including what will be the biggest fleet of 747-400s of any airline, (even eclipsing JAL).

From its early jet days using 707s and 727s, SIA now has Airbus, 757, 747 and A340s on the fleet, or ordered. This includes fifty-two 747-400 and 50 A340/E which will be delivered by 2003.

As well as their fleet modernity, SIA are famed for their in-flight service, which set standards others have had to emulate. SIA run their own ground operations at their Changi Singapore home base and also have three hundred world destinations on tap through their alliance with partners Swissair and Delta. Singapore Airlines' early regional services are now reflected in a strong regional network, but it is their ultra-long haul routes plied by 747-400 'Megatop' equipment that has made SIA a top long haul player.

It is the daily services from Singapore to London, New York, Frankfurt, Sydney and Los Angeles that are SIAs' blue riband flag carriers – taking the elegant blue and gold house colours into the heart of the airline greats and their territories.

The Singapore Airlines fleet comprises (or has on order) six A310s, seven A300s, fourteen 747-300s, up to fifty-two 747-400s, up to twenty-nine A340s, and thirty-one A340-300Es. The airline's base is Changi International Airport Singapore; its callsign is 'SQ'.

Operating one of the youngest airline fleets, SIA range far and wide from their Changi airport home. Here, under an Asian cloudscape, two 747s pass by.

ABOVE:
'Megatop' is the name SIA gave to the -400 seen here in profile and detail at Hong Kong as the Pratt & Whitney optioned -400 heads off to Changi in SIA's current golden colours. Note the droop of the fuel-laden wing – which will regain its dihedral in flight.

RIGHT:
Parked under the wings of a SIA 747-300 'Big Top', this Malayan Airways DC-3 marked SIA's fortieth birthday and really brought home the advances in aviation.

South China Sea Cruise. From 35,000 feet the blue of Asia was blinding – en route SIN–HKG on SIA.

Douglas delight. Snapped at rest, this DC-10-30 is resplendent in KLM's shiny blue. It's a classic shape that just yells 'heavy jet'.

LEFT:
Singapore style. 747-400 tailscape at Sydney.

ABOVE:
Catching the sun under stormy skies, the Kuwait Airways 747-200 gets towed up to the gate at a pristine Schiphol Amsterdam whilst KLM's blue birds look on.

RIGHT:
Double Bubble! This rare shape is the satellite communications housing fitted atop a certain security conscious Middle Eastern VIP 747 SP flight. Most 747SPs had Pratt & Whitney power, so this Rolls-Royce example, like its Qantas brothers, is a rarity.

Swissair sails in. Sinking into Hong Kong, this 747-300 of the Swiss national carrier is arriving from Zurich.

RIGHT:
Airbus moments. An Air France A300
spools up under a dusky sky.

BELOW:
Rarity value. One of the Iraqi green whale
fleet with their unusual livery design
makes ready to roll into take-off on
Heathrow's 27 right.

TWINS AND TRI-JETS

Whether it is an Airbus howling around the bend over Hong Kong or a Seven-Five-Seven whistling into Chicago, the big twins have made their mark. Pratt & Whitney, General Electric, Rolls-Royce, CFM, these are the names of the highly reliable 'big fan' engine makers whose engines power the big twins across the continents and oceans of the world.

With extended range EROPS giving up to 180 minutes' single-engined clearance, the big twins now have the world in their grasp. In fact, so well thought of has the concept become that a big twin probably has greater performance margins than the big tri-jets. With the advent of the Boeing 777 and the Airbus A330, the big twin has reached its ultimate, with weights (max. take-off) of 515,000 lb/223,600 kg, and 467,400 lb/212,000 kg respectively. The established tri-jet formula continues in the modified form of the MD-11 and its antecedent, the muscularly lined DC-10 series. The smoother contoured Lockheed L-1011 Tristar will remain an elegant sight for years to come, as will the smaller twins and tri-jets. With engine, re-engine, and airframe updates, the products of the 1960s and 1970s, the 727, the DC-9 and others will remain the classics that they are.

Seen here in the old and new colours of the airline world, the big twins and tri-jets and the people that fly, crew, and service them, are the core of the world's great airline moments.

Dragonair's stunning livery as applied to a 737-200, and seen as the baby Boeing scuttles across the Hong Kong ramp under the tails of other Asian carriers. First flown back in 1967, the 737-100s and 200s sold more than 1,100 examples with Pratt & Whitney JT8D power.

ABOVE:
This 767-200 belongs to Air China and looks workmanlike in its old-fashioned livery as it straightens up after the 'Kowloon turn' for a well-controlled sink into Kai Tak. First of the 767 family it weighs up to 387,000 lb, or 175,500 kg, in extended range version and can fly over 6,000 miles/12,600 km.

RIGHT:
Iberia's hard-working Airbus A300 fleet looks good in orange and white. Here an early variant howls into Heathrow on a stormy day. Despite its modernity, the A300 first flew in airline service way back in 1974. The -600 variant of the original Airbus A300 theme remains in production. Perhaps superseded by the A310 family with its composite components, new wing and updated avionics, the A300 remains a major workhorse and is the machine that made the sales break in the USA for Europe. (Not forgetting the Vickers Viscount, the Caravelle and the BAC 1-11.)

Late afternoon creeps up on Hong Kong in the form of this Airbus as she wheels her way around the turn. Note the generous flap and uninterrupted slat on offer.

BELOW AND OPPOSITE:
Tupolev Moments
Estonian Air is a newcomer. Here the
elegant Tu 134 rests at Amsterdam. Next, a
Malev Tu 134 looks more the old eastern
bloc part. Then, Balkan's 154 sinks down
the glidepath into Heathrow. Note the
unusual undercarriage.

OPPOSITE:
The old navigator/bomb aimer glazed nose of this early Tu 134 reveals its military design origins.

LEFT:
Australian Airbus. This rather smart A300B4 was caught spooling up at Sydney's domestic terminal. This one is GE-powered.

BELOW:
Winter sun casts a pale light on this Scandinavian 767 long-bodied machine as she creeps out of Heathrow.

ABOVE:
On African soil, a baby big-fan Boeing 737 in the rare markings of the Mozambican national carrier makes ready to depart Harare. Behind, an Air Zimbabwe 707 sweats out her old age.

RIGHT:
TAP Air Portugal operates Airbus minibuses in A320 guise on European routes. This one is just coming up to the gate at Heathrow's Terminal Two. Note the clean lines and wing box contours. Fly-by-Wire got bigger with the A340!

Rotate! Cyprus Airways heads home from Holland as its A320 screams off under computer-aided side stick control. Can't you just hear that distinctive A320 'whang' as the fans spin hard?

Taipei-based China Airlines use Airbuses on the Hong Kong shuttle. With her nosewheel turning and the engines running up, this A300 does a rolling take-off. Observe in this view the length of the undercarriage struts.

ABOVE:
A new Airbus of regional China Eastern skims into Hong Kong. This A310 looks busy with its extravagant livery and perfectly held pitch attitude.

Venezuela's VIASA descends on finals in
the classic DC-10 nose-up attitude –
helped by the authority of that huge, area
ruled, tailplane.

LEFT:
Spotters' delight! The MD-11 in Mandarin Airlines colours rolls across the Amsterdam ramp en route to Taipei. Note the winglets and reduced span tailplane – evident over the DC-10 predecessor.

BELOW:
Baby twin! An early 'hot rod' DC-9-20 built for SAS rests at Schiphol. This machine had the original DC-9 short body but with the addition of the slatted wing and bigger thrust of later models. Noisy, but effective.

RIGHT:
Crew at work. Here a Dutch Martinair DC-10 crew are captured preparing for flight.

BELOW:
Transavia is a long-established Dutch operator. Here one of its fleet of Boeings lifts off from Amsterdam with another load of sunseeking tourists.

ABOVE:
One of Air Zimbabwe's 737-200s rumbles across the Harare ramp after a flight from Victoria Falls. One of a family of three at Air Zim, she replaced an ancient but well-kept Viscount.

LEFT:
The main visual difference between the two big American tri-jets was the tail engine installation. This British Airways Tristar exemplifies the 'S' bend, faired-in technique that Lockheed used – as opposed to the DC-10's 'straight through the tail' engine duct. Concorde looks on!

This is another old stager – 727-200 belonging to the national airline of Jordan in its earlier colours. Note the large full span slats and stable, power-on approach.

LEFT:
The longest aircraft name ever? Bangladesh Bimans DC-10-30 *City of Hazrat Shah Makhdoom* (RA) takes a rest at Heathrow.

BELOW:
Gulf Tristar. Slinking off blocks at London, this is Gulf Air's night-time departure for Arabian lands. That golden falcon on the tail fin is now a visitor to LHR on the carrier's 767s.

ABOVE:
Japan Airlines called this a DC-10-40; seen here in the old JAL colours, it looks very smart indeed. This one is leaving Hong Kong for Tokyo Narita.

RIGHT:
Framed by the long span of a Lufthansa A340, this is Avianca of Columbia and its 'big orange' 767-200 ER getting ready to return to the sun.

TAILPIECES

Liveries reach their design heights on the tailfins of all the world's airlines. This is a selection of painted tail moments.

LEFT:
Boeing wash day! Two Boeings (a 747 and 727) get a wash and brush up from the folks at Hong Kong airport ground services. The 727 belongs to Emirates and has just undergone maintenance. Behind, Cathay make ready.

BELOW:
Tail Wars! A collection of images at Amsterdam.

ABOVE:
Olympic's Greek rings are an unusual example of classic-style airline livery design amid today's fashion for all white and all boldness. As you can see, this is an Airbus tail.

108

RIGHT:
Out in Africa, Air Zimbabwe's stripes sweat in the sun on the still stylish 707 tail.

ABOVE:
Bangladesh Biman DC-10 at rest.

RIGHT:
Photographed from the Amsterdam ramp, this Mandarin Airlines MD-11 is making a short stopover en route to Taipei. Note the Douglas 'straight through' tail-mounted engine.

RIGHT:
Iberia's mixed fleet of tails mix it with Lufthansa, Air Canada and a departing Speedbird in a classic moment.

Qantas kangaroo dominates the 747 tail
and the ramp at a sunny Sydney.